ALL THE LIFTERS

ALL THE LIFTERS

ESTHER MAZAKIAN

JOHN BARTON, EDITOR

Signature
EDITIONS

Cover design by Terry Gallagher/Doowah Design.

This book was printed on Ancient Forest Friendly paper.
Printed and bound in Canada by Marquis Book Printing Inc.

We acknowledge the support of The Canada Council for the Arts and the Manitoba Arts Council for our publishing program.

Library and Archives Canada Cataloguing in Publication

Mazakian, Esther, 1967–
All the lifters / Esther Mazakian.

Poems.
ISBN 1-897109-12-1

I. Title.

PS8626.A94A75 2006 C811'.6 C2006-905314-6

Signature Editions
P.O. Box 206, RPO Corydon, Winnipeg, Manitoba, R3M 3S7
www.signature-editions.com

For Levon and Shakeh, my parents

CONTENTS

BEAR THIS PRISTINE BRILLIANCE INSIDE

LITTLE MOULDY EXPLOSIONS

NOVEMBER PARTING DISASSEMBLY ENSUING ADULTEROUS STORM OF JANUARY ICE

ALL THE LIFTERS

HER LOST HIGHWAYS

BEAR THIS
PRISTINE
BRILLIANCE
INSIDE

Her Blanket Economies Niggardly In Search of Dire Depletions An Elusive Formula

Petrifying her depths every night, the blanket mathematics subverting
sleep, *eclipsing figures*, fixing the numbers to
render her
parents too young to die.
She would steal into their drawers in search of their survival formula,
after they'd fled, unconcerned with mortality, more concerned
with their
one night out,
that they'd italicize over and over for her benefit, *and the night was an eternity,*
so she'd morph into a mite
under
their bed to catch them falling asleep.
How did they lie? Bodies aligned in rest,
or coiled
unencumbered by hot blankets of sleep? Letting the slip
into the other side just happen?

Bombed and bereaved now, old phone numbers in her hands
instead of him,

she counted
the rings in the bedside table until her dream quit picking up his phone,
caller display,
and she counted down, counted on these dire depletions, *phone rings 3 . . . 2,*
go down, 2,
one
more rapid dark ride to zero,
and he knew it, *didn't he*, he knew that everyone leaves her
but he sent her away anyway;
so her remains migrated into the cold air
spectres inhabit outside
his house, *once their house*, cloaked and cold in his old

cardigan,
like in an empty person's skin, that she'd swiped,
her condensing breath dissolving into the

niggardly
silhouette he drafted
behind the curtains, *their curtains,*

his figure eclipsing her, her mind slipping into and she
listens for it
now, the night speaking again, *Shuffle the numbers*, dark
lines, black digits slurred
in her own
voice, *Do the math*
try to fend off the end go ahead but you're never coming back again never

With Moses Parting Her Red Watery Robe Again She Pinched Her Nose Inhaled Went Under And But

for shirking
a remarkable commotion of butcher paper
stuck
beneath her, she was safe.
Into a blue blackness that sent her back to the 1970s
back when her meekness belonged to her parents
and her body was harnessed in
by Eaton's:

navy pleats stopped
just under diapered aspirations, white
crepe blouse
beneath a baby
ensign blazer. Eyes pooling
woolly pools
of iris
regarding nothing
but the oily rainbow arcing unctuous over

their trinity:

her toy fingers curling
tentacles between her mother's as the swivel chair rolls
                                                  her father—sweaty
surgeon of his day—
to her.
After some 2000-odd years inside, Moses, delivered
into the cradle of waves before us, leaves her
system now.

Inside Her Darkest Ice Age

From under an avalanche of angst-y avoidance they sniffed out
an escape route like it was fresh kill; predators gathering in cool cahoots, they moulded
a smooth globular cake of icy guile
out of instinct, hard
snow, to serve as the first loveball of hot grade 8 infamy; a recess erection
for a week straight and architecturally,
a frozen
sherbet of near-

fornication
that caught her breathless one frigid morning ass-
first after Science, protesting disingenuous, gasping with hormonal semi-indecision,
her neck a scarf of sweaty mohair, her body a toppled
baby in a snowsuit, nylon arms, legs, hood pointed
into a star shooting toward the blue,
wintry,
cartoon-cloudy sky,
and her lips pressed to the lips of the maladjusted boy thrown at her
core, core of seedy pubescent entrails, boy from the back
of the class with the scuzzy
hair, plaque-hoary teeth, no wherewithal
to hand
anything in, and she kissed him hard, hard with a zealous, crural squeeze that surprised

even her, this boy, this boy that her mother
would have taken by the ear like a rat

by its tail
and fast chaperoned
out of her daughter's world, a world that was, until then, a still-frozen sluice of coming betrayal, that is,
before the cryo-

philic
father's head caught wind,
hacked up a squall of encroachment,
blew.

Charlotte Salomon Besieged

by nocturnal storms where no rain falls
but lightning strobelights the sky in a negative transfer
she shuts the windows
her Anne-Frank mouth dewing over
with thirst
purpling her lips sweet grape as she tastes her self
coaxed back into her stall

Our Hapless Ones

Uncovering a crime she'd
committed too,
Jocasta
loped disfigured backstage behind the ruins. Dreamt of school.
Ambushed and careening along the walls
of her nervous system, of
the conservatory at the university where they met,
she made
love with a face-
less Greek plumber in a disused bathroom stall. Choral odes extolled the bitter-
sweetness of her longing, a resown
field of desire
in the space between the air cells of her lungs.
Why should one look to the birds screaming overhead?

He left her and would again,
again. It was ordained.
So she ducked the furies, twisted the rope. Nowadays
she has no recollection
of anything before the Akin-
esia set in.

Her Pristine Seminal Texts Snake-Charming In Her In His Absence

This smell. Semen. Tapioca-white stains on her
palms, her stomach,
her breasts rising to meet him
in this almost lost fermata of memory—

urgent first drafts on cool amethyst mornings,
the duduk's snake-charming
autumn's apricot chrysanthemums
from their annular sphincters;
Dora then Cixous in quick succession,
timely ovulation, Medea crashing onstage again under pitting
pocks of scarring
hard rain;
Kurt Cobain;
spying pristine shoots of iris while abiding
a tenacious abstinence
in his absence. Medaglio d'Oro on the stove, hours-old ferrous tar soft as
the roving
new pavement of new sex sinking into her bones,
her breath
hooking a curl of glucose dipping
into the pillows and the sheets, linen coves of privacy,

wrapping dead daughters in this desire—

it hunted her like a debt; haunted her
like his bed; this age-old on-the-brink suck-in cure-all of lyrical brine;
it was life's fluid and it was viscous and it took.
Her first book.

Bear This Brilliance Inside

Orthopaedic chair, books stacked for weeks untouched
but rifled-looking. A polar
hibernating
headiness sealing her in her
master's hands. He was gone and she was yawing,
her balancing fingers thawing a crust of ice off the top of his desk—she bore this
hermitage inside like the pristine words he'd written,
eerie hieroglyphs across these
apartment walls,
classics carved into cranial bone.

Out the window a silent ischemic darkness

and her own italicized face,
his spy-
eyes on her metaphorically but still ablaze and on her
fate,
a spooky tree just bared for winter.

And Still Undertaking These Rites Rising Past Through These Formalities

Virulent and virtuous and well-preserved. Dessicated, shell-
acked carrion soul, haunted into haughty,
without any hope
of freeing the hosiery
from her
crotch, she eyed the other women escorted
into the long oaken pews
ahead
and she kept her gaze afloat as rites rose past and through her in waves of disdain
panic

nausea; they all knew her, that at her age
she could no more look eligible than she could flee these formalities.
Childless

and dross-eyed
in the back row—not hearing but searing in a blindsided inflammation of late arousal,
she touches her forehead
and she clears her throat
and she spies
all the rotting undertakers poised above her, still, gowns porcelain-
pale, chipped, lit, lips pursed as swilling aspirators
and a frantic series of regrets

and shame shutting her down one by one
as the old chorus
transports her

back to life
a last crazed effort to unearth her for a good laugh
watch this freak of nature greet the world's latest wife.

LITTLE MOULDY EXPLOSIONS

Little Mouldy Explosions In Their Daily Humidities How Like The Sight

Enormous and blackballed from the bird world ages ago adjusting her skinny legs her skinny head falling back onto the bed that kept her so far from the floor, kept her insomnia afloat. Her lips tight as an old woman's beak snapped shut in defiance after a hundred years of silence, her eyes bigger than the brain in her head on in the night like lights, lights on every night while she was showing the same show—black-in-white, swing-top wastebasket, almond toilet, sink, tub, brown face cloth folded into quarters and dank, *dank*, dank and ignored, *feared*, feared that if lifted a thousand centipedes would scatter in the rusty liquid. The towel that soaked up their shower splashes and weighed a ton like her, like the coming extinction she carried with her everywhere.

And she'd been there for centuries. She had the caulking around the tub memorized, the slammed and cracked wooden door, wood swelling as though something were hatching from within. She knew when the dust settled over the porcelain toilet-paper dispenser, the towel rack, the rim along the walls where the tiles stopped. And the peeling windowsill over the tub bubbling and glossed with residue all day long, exposing three paint colours beneath, the little mouldy explosions in their daily humidities that she knew like she knew the back of his head, the backs of his hands, the blight flowering between them. She'd been intimate with the hard-water stains around the shower rod, the iron deposits around the chrome taps, the grime, the black dirt she'd scoured and scoured like a mad housewife, and the night she crawled back to the bathroom in hysterics, feathers flying, not knowing what to do, grabbing a sponge and the dry cleanser, body shaking, powdery disinfectant blowing all over and into her eyes, a desert storm moving around her bird-head, the sand gritting her eyes as she scrubbed the bathroom clean.

That last night she got down on her knobbed knees and wiped the floor, lifted the brown face cloth she'd placed there to save the ceramic from water damage that in the end caused the water damage, she looked close at the grout lines and tiles rising, gently shattered from the moisture caught beneath, imploding as though if she were to peck through the mortar she would tap the pool of sewage brewing inside her and that night she brought the sopping towel and its mouldy, sour odour to the tip of her sharp nose and her skinny lips, her big stupid eyes peering at it as though it were his face, her bird-heart searching and heavy, sopping wet and heavy, *heavy*, heavy with a thousand hot showers, heavy with her coming extinction. It was always the night her tired forelimbs pressed her burning bird-head into the cold brown dank towel and left it there, hiding for the last time the belief that she could be unseen.

On that night of flight and fright that washed across her sand-gritted face, left it a blank screen projecting only that one show—the show about the hulking, hunkering ostrich blackballed and feared, *fearful*, feared and ignored, ignored instead of embraced. And *every night that night*, screened across her bedroom wall, the night her scarlet beak opened into a sharp V, her crazy clucking stopped and she shrieked, leapt, ran, her wings and legs flailing, her scrawny legs sprinting as unlikely as awkward as gawky as an old woman's knobby knees breaking backwards, needing to take flight but not, suspended, dancing in terror. And the dust settled over the ground of the bowlegged biped that night. Bird who used to be in proportion to her species, lost her place, ousted, shocked, as if under a shower gone cold. How like the sight of hysterics does hidden devotion seem, so that now, always, it would be the night he yanked her long skinny neck out from the dirt, refused to let her into his world again, turned her universe to dust, the night he swung her sloppy, sopping, fetid face cloth high, *high*, high on the rod to dry.

NOVEMBER
PARTING
DISASSEMBLY
ENSUING
ADULTEROUS
STORM OF
JANUARY ICE

i. Divorce

Absence fuelling an old pull towards privacy now;
was it *Feeling Gravity's Pull* sending her or was it this
existence
of contempt, necking
as she did with foreign bodies against rollicking barroom walls,
strolling off ledges of hard
anal sex,
the hangover/panic hurled headfirst at her in the day-
light—Bifurcator of the night, she was eating him
alive, gorging
on differences they used to joke
and gaze at each other
about in the day, when his blue eyes pale as pale were unsearching,
the feel of them on her still happy still unseeing
the reality of marrying a kinder father
instead of love.

ii. All Of Them Witches

How her desire was a November surge
of January sleet and how
whatever broke it could never interrupt its course.

How she hated him and his breathing
into her nape, a ventilator filtering useless hot air in and out
of her the sour dry odour
of his disgorged
pleasure. And how her mind rose above this marriage
and how she knew about him—
she rose and she knew and she flew
around the room, a ghost that read the rest
of the book he threw out, scribbled down his lies,
let the Scrabble tiles fall on the
black parquet and unlocked the anagrams, packed her hospital bag, as he fell,
came inside her.
Travelling the length

                                        of the hidden hallway, Rosemary tight-walked
the corridor behind the closet, knife held ice-pick tight,
unsedated on her course, ice-crushing
her nervous husband and his coven
of shrews.
                                                            Die for this?

Why die when the hideous earth was his and somewhere above Israel hers?

iii. Consort With Spirit

With a half quart of blended scotch,
a loveless life,
                                                  phantasmic, black-bearded, skin-tagged face
inside her,
face he boasted was not unlike the face
of Castro,
she sauntered
silly into the rehearsal party.
Staggering craggy daughter of a drunken bastard long exiled from this crowd,
she was soused like him, sullen like him,
single like he never was. And she wished she had a wife like his.
A woman as still as a vigil as the room of tubes strung him up,
hoisted him back from every infarction
as though transporting a great animal through the air,
animal incurable and absent as a dictator,
animal unable to anticipate migration on its own.

UP

                         to the makeshift bar, a makeshift bartender, she licked
her whetted lips at the best man—*best*, indeed—
unpruned swilling virtuoso,
stirring her bones like the ice in her glass, two shakers
                                                  going above his ears like the silver martini maracas
of a sly,
hollow-legged
angel watering her drinks down down down to make them last—

iv. In Noir Transit

It was as though the cruelties of entomology led her to him.

On an acrid, fly-by-night lark,
she went to bed with him and his heartbreaking
hair dyed ash blonde and rank.
And the flow,
the low
criminal flow of moisture
between them submerged her even when
her indecision was pressing
then lifting her body
and her psyche
was home laughing away this humiliation—but since when should shame paralyze her?

CUT

to this boy in her film,
the scene where there was a subway turnstile between them, station altitude
aerial
and cirrous as his hair when he'd motioned to her,
wings spread
like red game in her world of black and white,
his puerilia licking into a shadowy backdrop as she happened by, beaming, placed her
hands in his.

v. Missileman

Admittedly a bit scrofulous, even by her own new leftist
estimation, she admitted to everything then left her husband, as
conservative,
as incidental, as always, in the black bed-
room, horrified,
deflated, and as usual,

laryngitic.

In the hall closet listening
to this boy's voice on her phone; if it were possible
to absorb the receiver
into her ear,
brain,
crotch, well then! she would have; his hot, collusive spin
on the facts that made sexy-ironic sense,
his rewriting the news
of impending
war;
laying velvet carpet bombs and rubbing her against his
attitude, she was for
then against him every
night these
days, two stammering pundits swallowing tongues long into the night.

Ubiquitous rush of him passing her up the stairs, she grabbed her bag
then down,
down and out the door and across

the street,

into the car and via chevrons arrowing the minutes back to skirting

issues, rimming the heady perineal dirt
of duplicity between his
legs
digit
by recidivist
digit then digging her in it in it in it in it

vi. Singe This Bliss

She loved.
The hollowness of lust. Greed. Fasting. Driving hungry
at night then dropping
barren and on fire into his bed.
He was wrenching
through her, singeing her lungs, ovaries, intestine,
reparation—
her phoenix perfectly inextinguishable.
And she loved the diaphanous pleasure, their embraces
tense as their adultery, as the Romans rushing in to rob them of this bliss—
she loved it, she loved him, she loved
that it was a finger-snap away,
this betrayal,
turning on the single-pistil, five-toothed calyx
redbud
of her family tree.
Wrapping him in her dress. She clasped him to her breasts, hopeless,
whispering that battered cliché into his ear night after

destitute night,
You are what you are what you are.

vii. Their Etched Ocular Ice Storms

With an indecisiveness that had already decided her fate
she spent the season buying nothing
but a spree of cocktails
and subterfuge.
The only
tiny white lights she beheld was the rush pouring
                                        over, scanning them from beyond
the etched ocular sockets of Modigliani's girls on his apartment walls.

And her own eyes were vibrating
at the sight;
splayed, balls blown glass, skin shimmery
tinsel, his knees shuddering
on the burnt umber couch, pressing her—

                        But now trim the tree back home.
Mantel-line incoming cards. Pretend sex
isn't frozen outside the kitchen window in a Montreal ice storm of her suspended
moisture. That this treachery
of tongues was a dream;
Faustian tar seeds of vanilla peppering,
                                milking the lips

of the wasted.
Clear drop of a foot-long icicle dipping off the eave made her gasp.

ALL THE LIFTERS

Spring Storm

Thanks
to a blustery disruptive wind, rain fell
sideways and hit the porch in clean intervals,
as though on a timer. Racing
to the bedroom to shut the window,
she witnessed lightning strike the tree next door,
a giant limb crack, drop,
the cable line loosen, swing.

October. And her mind drifted
to last spring when she turned thirty and officially

traded places with her father. A knack for saying the wrong thing, she rode
a liquor rampage like a twister lasting
weeks, flew at people in floods
of disorder,
ululent—

Lights flitted past. Pulse tore through her. After thirty
years
she was still afraid

of the rain, the trees that arched heavy,
straightened, leaned
back again.

Snapped. And her mind cried
out for the wind, for the wind to stop,

just let it *stop.*

Internal

We drained it last time, he told her coming out
from between her legs. But we'll take another
ultrasound find out what's going on
in there.
She blinked into the neon flooding her eyes,
hot sun glaring over the expanse
of her body.
Blood clots seeped out of her
like blasted jelly
fish washing
onto shore,
while she beheld a constellation of shiny stains
freckling the black pools
in her head. Where she spotted her father,
dauntless heavenly body,
explosive, thin
skinned father swimming back again

                                        to set up the tripod,

scream and bitch,
make an overcompensatingly zealous sprint
to his spot
behind her before
the timer goes off.

All The Lifters

She remembered faces like a negative.
Especially
her father's faces. So
it would never have gotten past her, his lying
and the other woman's face;
they were more than photogenic;
they lit the screen in an epileptic flash of recognition.
She knew about the women, she knew him
as well as she knew herself:
the sun soaked up their skin with the same urgency,
and the moles that peppered her body peppered
his as though he'd seasoned her.
Their fingers and legs were lean:
his curly hair fell heavy
and black down her back.
Time was he'd lift her into the air and toss her,
making her laugh for the camera.
And she loved falling into him,
the neat fit of him that was not her mother. So thrilled falling
into him, her arms would lift,
lift with a fear pure,
groundless,
and her body would tremble

with panic,
delight at the sight of his face out of time, coming in, going out,
coming in to her,
her wet mouth open in a V—
She'd fallen into his life by accident. So
she learned to remember everything,
learned early about the women
he picked up, how to capture their faces
before they were gone. To be a woman, his to toss
in the air, unafraid,
free, *free*, free-for-the-taking.

Fierce Cannibals

It had just rained and they brought their umbrellas
for nothing because the sun was coming out
to offer up the last of the day.

Shopping for dinner—
they laughed randomly at random things they said
and when he turned to cull a head of broccoli
from the crowds of produce
she looked at the back of his and loved it
though she knew it held fierce
to a sort of natural
selection;
a self-preservation that cut her
out of the running. As he glutted on parts
he savaged about him, bloodied
global economies soaring,
prices set too high for the starving she suddenly reared,

SAVE ME—

He sang all the way home to cover her silence
and she nearly cried out for a downpour,
for the late afternoon that she knew
would end and did.

Sun

Passing in and out of daylight
is the work of the surviving.
As though widowed,
she goes down, loses her breath,
re-emerges again
into the light.

She never did ask him for anything,
but he walked and talked around her for weeks
as though she had. This
manipulation being serious business,
she had him arrive again and again, his bookbag hanging
against him, his hair golden, his lips
mouthing just-in, up-to-date, sorry-this-is-how-
it-is explanations
to make her crazy.
She turned away from his nape, man-
suetudinal flesh that she'd held up to the hot sky once like Medea en-
raptured,
and she went back to the headiness that comes
when she buries herself

under his pillow,
where she finds the coolness of the earth.

You are not *my wife*, he said to her.
Unsurprised,
but still somewhat murderous,
Let me tell you *something,*
she quoted a line from a scary movie:
'a son is a poor excuse for a lover'.

So, get her another drink, Son
and when you leave
leave for good,
take the sun with you.

Cherry Gum

Every night she grasped the suede shoebrush he left behind,
but the other way round. The soil-stained
two-sided brush—steel-bristled on the one side,
knobbed on the other—
was what she held on to, what prickled
the inside of her hand,
while the flat brown plastic end, shaped
like a teardrop,
lightweight, silent
functional, entered her, engraved
with the gold word *Tana*
and before long began to take on
the odour of the plastic used to make cheap Barbies.
The ones she'd hold to her nose and inhale
under the covers
because they smelled like cherry gum.
Dolls her brother used to dare her to swipe from him,
waving them over her head like candy; yes,
yes, cool flossy hair tickling
her eyelashes,
shucked-off blonde trichome sprouting
from heads she'd roll later

in the palm of her hand, a born lone
driver shifting gears. So even at age 8,
she knew where to find them—
the masters mould man-made materials
for bait—
and how to inveigle
what she needed from what they handed down.
Legs long, smooth, pliable,
stood her own hair on end, flamed
her cheeks, rubbed
her by proxy,
love and marriage and children raised in strokes
for and against the grain
of her napped flesh,
the soft suede inside that had him coming
back to her every night in waves, back and forth, to and fro, in and out, and in

Transport

With hopes of reaching the edge of the world
she walked and walked,
alone, up and down the streets, passing
the same stores, the same garbage, the same
menu boards, the same men
smoking outside the same restaurants.
Was it coincidence
that every time she struggled against
the sun up that one hill, the moment she passed
JASON BLOWS DEREKS
COCK in magenta on the concrete
bridge wall, the head
of a subway train nosed up
from underneath the earth
like an old friend, to say hi, to see her,
knowing she was on her way?
It transported her every time
to when she used to wave madly,
when waving at inanimate objects as they
stormed past was reasonable.
Or maybe it was hope,
that the train saw her waving? Or

that it would stop?
When conversation was unsullied
by what was said and there was only
a line between
desire and swallowing
the world. And her mouth
could never outrun her;
she was friends with everything, promise
was Promise and her mother was poking
the windshield at the bridge, *Look! There
goes the train, Baby!*
and not making out what
her mother was pointing at but waving
anyway, laughing, calling, *Bye bye
train! Bye!* watching nothing
except the back of her mother's head
and her own left hand squeezing
the burgundy headrest. In love
with the button poking out from underneath
that made it move. Deep red
rest stopped,
she made sure, at
the right spot so her mother could
rest her head, though she never did,
but there just in case
she needed to.

HER LOST HIGHWAYS

Paramount Pictures

What a complicated system
this industry
her brain
that kept his skeleton
                                encased body alive
                    unaffected by the exposure
                                                    years his flesh was bombarded
scanned
through by the charged fluorescence behind her closed lids
    lucky
bedsprings coiled
at differing degrees beneath him
nightly storms of light the flesh and bone on the other
side of life
    the length of her room the length that held her
anticipation
          at its end the face that was luminous his face radiating a film
of heat
      his mouth
saliva leaking out
his nostrils coming inspiring pure

red purple blue purple crimson pumping
oxygen
sleep
          or an unconquerable disregard only she could dream up a text
x-ray of white diffracting into black covert
shirts
checked, denim, ox
blood boots macerating Monty into John Wayne.

Lobby

Succulents retaining water on the windowsill, I'm ready, she asserts,
                    breasts swelling, while he shoulders
an axe in the hallway undecided. Seduction doesn't work on him anymore, not

since
he used to fight with his father for hours
about Israel, believing in him and subsequently thwarted by how he could transform so
triumphant just stepping into the adjacent room; Arab then Jew, Arab,
his father was a public official, a slippery-eyed
clandestine
prick, occupying his every movement, centuries-old entitlements, not

                              unlike this adultery plowing
into her pillows, pushing him through this downpour, Israel moving deeper
into the West Bank,

she's needle-nosed and beautiful beyond this door,
                              she's as cowering as a search-
light surging
through shark-calloused waters, as one more soldier's circling campaign before
the strike.

Some Nerve

Real pain. Palms flush and on his stomach to straighten his spine, ease
the pressure weighing on the nerve the herniated
disk was pushing
against,
disk lodged not unlike a shotput,
the one
she'd whipped at the small of his back sometime weeks before when she told him she
loved him.
Piercing lasso instead of the friendly shock
absorber
his body needed, ached
for. For real? Was he joking? Should she call someone? She raced to the freezer,
grabbed
the first thing that felt big enough to cover burning
vertebrae, lifted
his striped pajama top he'd been ailing in for weeks, the couch
to his bed, bed to the easy chair, sitting, lying
gingerly
as though
impaled,

and she lay the frozen chicken breast and pressed, leaned over
him
holding but he kept wailing, voice louder
Oh my sciatica scaring her *Your what?*
she flung a leg over,
straddled

but with her thighs not touching him, a position purely incidental,
unribald,
what anyone would do
                                        in an emergency

and she pressed her breast into his back only wanting to end
the pain really
push it through the kitchen linoleum
where he'd fallen
like a man made of timber,
                    a stretch of weeping wood, legs logs, moaning she was
sure for her to yank the radiating pulse out of him and replace it with her
cool meat.
                    But she didn't know how. To snap on latex.
Perform the protocol to save him. Knew he was screaming for her to get off. Knew
sooner
that what he needed was his mother
to bend over and pick him up
in her arms body supportive as a lumbo-sacral brace, heart a hot compress,
soul a deep
massage.
                                        Knew pressing
her icy breast into him was the worst thing
to do
                                        as the paramedics told her when they came
and took him away. Knew it was about her
not him. Knew.

Pinned At Last By John Ashbery

Overhead the curtain
rod was laced
gossamer by a wonder-crochet of spider-netting, under-
pinnings that held this apartment up, tiger
cub
by the nape. He raced the porch steps, turned at the trellis, exited the frame
of their window.

Wrenching her dense hair round her palm into
a pug
between her pituitary wings,

anxiety found her
a road back to that tired remorse and its dull ache inside her
addled and pining way after seven years she still didn't know
where the postal outlet was
where

he picked up
the packages she ordered
online. Cleaners. CIBC. How

to breathe
when he embraced her, hot fingers
through an agoraphobic network
of her cross-grating nerves. She squinted at the mantle. Scratching revising editing publishing

of all the blinding galley proofs of defection
didn't help—
get a paper
circle ads
call for appt.'s

MOVE

Why Call Them Death Dreams This Running This Running This Wind?

i.

Icy hands,
one of the hazards of reading on a made bed—
in one movement, still
curled,
creeping under
the covers, the hot cloud fabric
falling over her knees so that it was as though she were lying
beneath herself, she finally slept again.
Either you take on characteristics of the victim,
or the aggressor, or neither, or,
as in her case,
both. Dreams dash by trees
smudged across rubber-rimmed subway windows.

ii.

Why do you call them Death Dreams?
her therapist asked the dead air
in her left-
handed voice.
He gave me life, filled me. Now I'm nothing. You know, do you know
how I feel on the subway
after I leave here?

iii.

Tulips tower, slip through the lips
of their stalks.
She followed him around everywhere,
accepted every utterance he let slip
from his lips.
He was her brilliant tower
until the slow
surprise of accumulated compliance
siphoned his hold
and before she knew it, carried her
downstairs where her voice soared
into the air vents, into the city
that was their room
where he listened on their bed, thwarted
father
of a fulsome, foul-
some child.

iv.

Along with a break-up comes the realization
that people shift to camps. So,
not surprisingly,
alone in her new attic apartment she sat dreaming
against walls closing in (no furniture),
windows shutting out outside (no drapes).
I want you
out,
said over and again because she would never believe it.
Drive the point home, she sang, laughing
at the joke,
then crying
her own elegy into his sweater
as the soil flew between them. How she'd emptied
her soul with decision.

v.

On the first anniversary clothes materialized
from garbage bags, wrinkled,
cold, the stripped-off clothing
of victims,
carrying only the smell of the bags
they were thrown in
in haste.
Pant legs unfolded. Angry shirts blossomed from tight fists.
Sweaters, the regulars
and the disused, congregating
strangers in a catastrophe collapsed onto the floor.
Undercover,
duty-bound, ready for work, the starving
yet still alive someone stashed
behind the panelling
in time
from the massacre. When her army had seen worse.
She'd packed her Armenian babies, her
father's glasses,
journals,
all her glottal anguish,
the harrowing hoarfrost that stitched her lips, and she *left*.

vi.

Funeral weather is necessarily
windy. Air moves in a bluster to muster
up the scent, push
against stone markers, reiterate
positions.
And she died three times
last night, again, every night awash in vanishing light, driving home
the point.
Why do you call them Death Dreams?
                                        When her father
died, a stone
where he once was, it was so windy the trees knew
about her
and she ran
from the black family mourners
and she slammed the green car door,
her own grey head buried
and foundering into the forest upholstery,
her panic thinning
eyes shutting at the same time she wrested them open,
she began her life inside

this breathing
paradox

box.

Listen:
The contradiction of sleep is dream's traffic.
So death, she asked the rivulets
coursing through the old stucco-white ceiling abrasions, *wasn't it the same rivetting effort to wake?*

vii.

It's hard to assimilate after you
have lived a lifetime
with God.
Crazies congregate cleverly,
separately,
on subway cars,
that way no matter where she sat
they stationed themselves
nearby. It was three
years since he made her leave and every maniac
in the city
could see it. Memory shattered her
face, efflorescent, blooming
hangover face, a gauge measuring
time
without him,

                                        the rest of her
frame sucked in reverse,
her presence wrenched from his side into this idling dream-
life, a diminishing slow-moving
hearse
of unconsciousness.

Lost Highways

Run
through books from the end, endings should arrive without
surprise—not marry unless
you can divorce him first.
                                        Whoever *him* is.

Run
the elastic taut, see that it is red, nightmarish. Migration
casts you
                whether you're a bird or some marble-eyed
disassociated
fish, from father to this.
                                Whatever *this* is—an identity crisis,

neurologically, *this* may be a
migraine,
believed to be excessive
expansion and contraction of blood
vessels
in the brain, blind
surgings,

you had your first at 4, your father's hands
spotting you
                    on the monkey bars. The soft underside
of paternity raising you
up,
your soft core soaring.

Run afraid of seizure, or is it the egression of metaphor, orgasm,
strange otiose structures
of desire.
Lynchian blue-velvet interiors course frenetic
along arteries splitting you
in two,
dark highways Bill Pullman-esque,
or speeding
scared
scared you may actually stop, get some rest.

Green Rancour In The Hushed Resilience Outside Waning As If For Spite

Radiant energy and light and photosynthesis
so essential
as to be mocking, spring shot up
from the ground, tulips leapt
into her arms, glorious, red,
their sudden headstrong rancour for sleep strong

as his insistence
on dying this past fall
after he darted behind the drapes
and she darted too, when her deter-
mination alone would kill his feline indifference.
Spring was no solace;
she'd fought arrangements,
brought him back home from the hospital to bathe him
herself, clear the litter
burring his coat, apply the post-

surgical cream to the eczema on his
belly, cradle his perfect body, a furred embodiment
of her lifespan, while his eyes
nearly callous

and green, green waning into yellow, yellow waning
to spite her,
his stubborn interloper, choking
his stiff limbs in hers, his paws
padding
her hair, her cheeks, her lashes

but inadvertently;

his life was not to care for
the sorrows of those,
those who search for solace in the grass, pull
wings off living flies of fire, procrastinate
examinations, appointments,
fresh water,
little

shits who, whenever they get the chance,
burn cigarettes into the hushed resilience outside

and test the limits of pain.

A Passing Homage to Jane Kenyon

At the window—
it sounded like the wind,
but it was a car passing over
the snowy road.
Bare limbs under street lamps
looked more like roots. In the distance, moving
clouds coming out from behind
buildings were puffs of smoke rising
off a smoldering fire.

She carried her drink carefully up
the stairs so as to not rouse the hour,
the stillness. A soporific spell
had settled on the world and somewhere
inside her finally believed that what she thought she knew
about herself,
the clouds,
didn't mean much.
Winter brought spring,
outside brought her insides some comfort,
and the disgrace that kept her awake
would end,

then suddenly rain—
morning may come but sleep never will.

Ravish Me In Jackets Red Hyacinth White Your Small Hands Of Rain

Flowers with itineraries, tulips
bring spring in to her
whether or not she's conscious.
Erect and stalwart,

sexcups
that later fall open, un-tulip-like, they expose their inner
machinations,
stamens outstretched
and headed like the body of the man she loved.
Sweet, unspeakable
absence

underground that peeled her away and back slowly,

surely,

a radicular strip-
tease,
tuberous ecstasy in his comings like frail fingers raining all over her
arms and a yellow talc dusted her shins then

and she trembled,
I gave up the discourse of love. Please,

don't, she told the falls swooning at the gate, Wasn't love's

euphoria
another buried spasm, engorged
hyacinth,
same anxiety that can erupt in murder, or in a sly hush, usher in lush
springtime amnesias?

Acknowledgements

I would like to thank the following magazines for publishing work from this collection, some in earlier forms and under different titles: *Arc*, *CVII* , *The Danforth Review*, *Event*, *The Fiddlehead*, *Gaspereau Review*, *The Malahat Review*, *PRISM international*, and *Pagitica.*

"Lobby" was an Editor's Choice in *Arc*'s 2002 Poem of the Year Contest. "Ravish Me…" and "Her Seminal Texts…" won the Earle Birney Prize for Poetry in 2004, awarded by *PRISM International.* Thank you to the editors there, especially Elizabeth Bachinsky for her kindness.

Much gratitude for the support and generosity of the Toronto, Ontario and Canada Arts Councils, which always seemed to arrive in the nick of time.

Special thanks to:
Mom and Dad, there no matter what, thick, thin; Hasmik, my dear, long-suffering sister, and Hagop, my brother, and their respective families for their help, interest, encouragement, not always in the poems, but always in me.

The sound air of Dr. Mavis Himes and her well-timed kicks in the ass, 'navigating the moisture and the inactivity.'

Wayne, so constant, with love and thanks. Netty, Buddy, my babies.

And John Barton, my editor, for his intuitive mastery, his availability, his faith in my tensile, wavering lines.

Notes on some poems:
The quotation from "Our Hapless Ones" is from *Oedipus Rex* by Sophocles. "Fierce Cannibals" and "Sun" are for my long-time friend and re-friend, Sean Turunen. "Green Rancour…" is for Luka. "Lobby" sprang from a passage in the memoir, *Misgivings*, by C.K. Williams. The line "small hands of rain" from "Ravish Me…." is derived from a line in e.e.cummings's poem, "somewhere I have never travelled."